MW00379208

GENDER FLYTRAP

Sundress Publications • Knoxville, TN

Copyright © 2019 by Zoë Estelle Hitzel
ISBN: 978-1-939675-92-7
Library of Congress: 2019946689
Published by Sundress Publications
www.sundresspublications.com

Editor: Erin Elizabeth Smith
Editorial Assistant: Anna Black

Special thanks to Maria Esquinca, Erica Hoffmeister, Jenna Jankowski, Annie McIntosh, Jacquelyn Scott, and Eva Weidenfeld.

Colophon: This book is set in Bell MT.

Cover Art: "Gender and Mirrors" by Tara O'Nay (taraonay.com)

Cover Design: Kristen Ton

Book Design: Erin Elizabeth Smith

GENDER FLYTRAP
ZOË ESTELLE HITZEL

ACKNOWLEDGMENTS

Some of these poems have appeared previously in the following publications:

Blue Lyra Review: "Gender Dysphoria versus the February Skyline"
The Chariton Review: "Silent Shout" (as "Truth Salad, Movement 1")
Entropy: "Insomnia—Bird"
The Fourth River: "Male Bonding"

I thank the editors and readers of these magazines for supporting my work and providing it an audience and for keeping literature alive in an American culture which values other pursuits and appears to have an endless supply of too little time for the things that make life worth living.

Table of Contents

The Jerry Springer Show, Therefore I Am

Male Bonding

Gender Dysphoria versus the February Skyline

The Azalea Princess

"You don't get to have a mind without a body. They're the same thing."
                                        -Eula Biss

"The worst injury is feeling you don't belong so much to you."
                                        -Claudia Rankine

"…and I imagine what is dark and incomparable passing between us / like a dialogue between mirrors abandoned…"
                                        -Louis Aragon, "Poem to Shout in the Ruins"

"I am alive in myself / born to birds / who spoke a language / that never fit me. / So I say girl. / So I say woman. / So I say body. / This is the best I can do for now."
                                        -Joshua Jennifer Espinoza, "Affirmations"

The Jerry Springer Show,
Therefore I Am

First

1.

the rustle on carpet

she squirms deeper

in the bedsheet fort

to shadow her teacup

pupils black and brimming

a radiant television midnight

upstairs the parents

sleeping gods

the weight of their steps

the weight of their silence

she wraps herself in

blankets like secrets

a clip of moonlight could betray

she is still

the fort is still

the moon careens around the far side of the planet

pretending safe in the dark

a word from the television

catches in a nameless

terra incognita clutch of herself

a distance agape and tremored

darting, dilated eyes

and the world snaps

quick as a window

spiderwebbed by a pebble

2.

blue screenlight flickers
an image of women

bodies propped onstage
to curse kinesthetic

while a wire antennae
transmits the shapes

of their angst their ardor
the colors of stardust

made meat and slapped
at birth with a label

and taught to trust the slapper:
if you have any doubts,
look down

Jerry's audience snaps
their words as one
whipcrack possessed of ancient tradition

and Steve leaps onstage from off camera to force
himself between guests hurling insults like fists

and fists like insults and Jerry says nothing
in the bright hot studio chanting his name

Jer-ry! Jer-ry!

creases his brow
to perform concern

brandishes cue cards
to perform order

offers his mic
to perform benevolence

and the audience accepts
his silent invitation

to prod the guests
and their miserable pieces

the unruly breasts
spilling from push-up bras

the stark foundations
peppered with stubble

the mineral baritones
wrapped in lace chokers

the wigs yanked off
and hurled like grenades

all the miraculous fishnet shapes
curved against each other

and Steve leaps onstage from off camera

3.

her fort fills blue
with television laughter

the people as bodies
the bodies as freakshow

she fits herself into

the wrong she understands

a tree's brittle hiss fills the cruel night air

a silence slips over the word in her skull

she fidgets the volume down

Ghosts

her mouth did not notice
the word press her tongue
against her teeth the word
opened and pursed
her lips the word honed
her breath to sibilant
and fricative and she recognized
vaguely a distance
within her crying the word

she had no words
to know why she watched
Jerry night after blue night

or words for why the word
obsessed yet repulsed

or words for why instinct
shrouded her quiet

hidden and dark
she licked at her silence
the ghosts in her body awake

The Thought

The body
is a mouth

around me. I study
the cavity. Lips

slash open in a torrent of light.
Shape the word *woman*.

Somebody talks.
It isn't me.

I don't want to know who is talking.

Why am I here with this huge bright word?

Its echoes digest.
I wither in the glare.

Sprint the dry tongue.
Leap into a shadow.

Whisper, *no*.

Hope to be just another
sound, a shiver
between teeth.

Four Portraits of Revelation

1.

Habit drew her anointed fingers
to forehead, chest, and shoulders, left first, then right.

Habit muttered in obedience or worship
then gave her voice to god.

Habit's obligate reverence ascended
a chorus everyone pretended to know.

Habit bent necks to hands that knew
when to fold and when to open.

2.

She underwent a holy sacrament.
Received a white leather bible.
Ran her finger over the soft gold-leafed edge.
Then the giver whispered, *masturbating*
wastes perfectly good babies.

Sex class offered two options:
Contract a crotch disease!
Or prove yourself to god
via purity, chastity, deference, the body
a moldering temple someone else had furnished.

3.

Her parents' bright home smelled graham cracker sweet.
Jesus hung bloody above doorways.
God listened to everyone's thoughts like the NSA.

4.

When her fingers knit and the words she had learned
to say with full heart and closed eyes moved through her
she wondered, Was she good enough?
To ask for help? To receive it?

She asked god for a Nintendo
instead of the body
she could not trust.

She didn't get it.

Math Problem

Definition: You gather *sex* means one of two and only two
bodies you can be, and *the body* determines
everything—identity, dreams, love, the future,
where you pee, what people say when you cry.

Given: You are told you are male, that you have a male body.
You are told these things as if they are the same.

Corollary 1:   Since you have a male body, it is assumed you love people
with female bodies, which should act as further evidence
supporting your dubious maleness.

Corollary 2:   Without romantic experience, you assume whom you love—
and therefore who you are—based on what bodies tend to be
prettier.

Figure One: You have *a male body*,
Figure Two: and you know *your body*
Figure Three: tells you *it needs to be female*
Figure Four: and is *freaking out.*

Consider: Which weighs more, a ton of feathers or a ton of gravel?

Directions: None.

Show your work: *Needing to embody female physiology,*
the concept, makes sense—
like a fear of hornets makes sense
or letters assembling into words makes sense

or pulling the blankets tighter when you're cold makes sense—
and makes no sense at all.

The thought most often appears unannounced
to dangle in the mind for minutes, like needing to eat.
It blares large and insistent.
Strickens like a coughing fit.
Nudges slight as a snowflake melting on a glove.
A splinter. A kiss. Burnt toast for lunch.
Standing in a ballfield gaping at a passing plane

(Over):   disappearing into the blue summer.
It coruscates longing.
Binds and suffuses.
The body like an edict.
Always the thought
leaping from a corner
to flashdance the center of awareness.

Rationale: You guess *transsexual* may explain
how an absence can feel so present.

Extrapolate: Slowly the cataract noise
will condense to cloud
all other thought.

Final Answer: <u>I will ignore this until I cannot.</u>

Sexing the Body

The thought became a small sun
glowing in her skull.

She beamed at magazine lesbians
and imagined she was one of the sweaty women

squinting through kohl-lined eyes.
The first time, she wore a silver brassiere

and stared in a mirror, caressing the silver
lightning which shot from her shaven thigh,

imagining what it would feel like
to have those collapsed cups filled.

Dial-up Internet—Quiz

She asked who she was and found quizzes.

Do you ask for directions when lost, or keep driving?
Is parallel parking difficult?
Do you ever park in reverse?
Would you consider yourself handy?
Can you install speakers?
Do you follow directions when assembling furniture?
Do you prefer working with people or on your own?
How accurate is your passive orientation to the cardinal directions?
Do you prefer to please others, or to have others please you?
Do you grow your hair out? How long?
Do you clip your nails, bite them, or file them down?
Which of the following skincare products do you regularly use?
Boxers, briefs, or panties?
Liquor, beer, or wine?
How often do you shower?
Do you ever take baths?
Where do you shave?
Do you own makeup?
Whom do you find attractive?

Now add up your responses—you are the answer.

Dial-up Internet—Fantasy

1.

she searched for herself and found Chicks with Dicks! Slutty Shemales! Live Tranny
Action! Simpering Transvestites! Submissive Ladybois! Primped, Horny, and Waiting
for You! to hurry up with the easy payments and check the Yes I Am Over 18 box and
click past the popups and neon marquees to get to the hot-hot-hot

2.

she revised her search terms and Lycos or AOL or Geocities found her forced
      feminization erotica

she dove into fantasy stuffed with hyperfemme outfits too girly for the girliest girls,
      facials, manipedis, waxing, updos, deportment and voice and handwriting
      lessons, the pinkest bedrooms, the fluffiest plushies, tea parties, bubble baths,
      lisps—girlhood taught to boys as taboo, imposed as potent antidote

then scifi: electrolysis, hormones, piercings, laser, impossibly elaborate surgical facilities
      built to make boys be girls by remaking their bodies

then magic: enchanted salons whose seats rooted you in place when they knew you
      wanted bangs and a makeover but couldn't ask

the transformations masterminded by lusty Dominants whether the transformed
      enjoyed them (sometimes) or not

some protagonists knew the masculinity they'd learned to wear though it never quite fit
      a façade built atop their reluctance to explore the feminine they'd learned to fear

her body, loudly: *stay a while*

3.

her body fought its male puberty
with role play kink and echo
whether she wanted it or not

but nobody came to whisk her away
from the body her body was becoming
whether she wanted it or not

Dial-up Internet—Diagnosis

1.

She browsed for *Why* and found psychosis and malaise.

Fetishistic transvestite: Your taste in clothing is the illness.

Autogynephilia: Your arousal is the illness.

Gender identity disorder: You are the illness.

Was she a *false transsexual*, a gay male liar abusing medical goodwill to fulfill a sex fantasy?

Or a *true transsexual*, with true suffering, truly deserving of medical attention?

Was she real enough? To be believed?

Was she *born in the wrong body*, like the *Jerry* women said? Were they *true*? Were they *false*?

She scratched at her junior high moustache and her junior high boner withered.

She did not find any diagnoses for wanting to be a man but she had seen *The Silence of the Lambs* and *Ace Ventura: Pet Detective* but not *Sleepaway Camp* or *The Crying Game*.

She was a diagnosis for wanting to embody *woman*.

And what was *woman* but something she shouldn't want to be?

2.

She deleted her history. Cleared her cache.
Made a folder in a folder in a folder in a folder
full of decoy folders labeled random keystrokes
nested in decoy nests. She gathered
photographs. She gathered the afflicted
were meant to be treated
with straight jacket cinches
and cured.

Black Velveteen Opera Dress

Sunlight through blinds shimmered the fabric
and lit her beneath it, floating her secret

afternoons aglide over stone and imagined ice
dancing with something like her body.

The softest softness clung to her shape.
The socks stuffing her bra reshaped her.

She kept a pile of stolen laundry
beneath a white wooden dresser under a cross.

She dressed in the basement and listened for footsteps,
jangle of keys on door, floor creaks, cabinets.

She wanted to resemble *what my body knows*
and clothes helped her feel *less like I am.*

Her parents found the pile, and father erupted
"Are you a faggot?! Don't lie. No son of mine…"

Mother, irate, invoked her god
to condemn the devil's child, punish the thief.

Blood thinned. Cheeks flushed. Heart rocket. Nervequake.

She did not know what to say, or how

so they might understand her trying to understand her relationship with this
    body that has its own mind–will–identity–knowledge separate from her and
    unified and screaming
without sounding quite insane.

The sweat collected in her collar.
The sweat dripped down her leg.

She became the sweat escaping her body.
She became *what is wrong with you*.

Male Bonding

Phallocentrism with Swimsuit

Father sips Budweiser in grandmother's dining room.
Shirtless and fit, swim trunks short
to display his gargantuan runner's thighs
balanced atop splinted shins he called chicken legs.

Dad! Dad! I figured it out!

I am a child with swimsuit
in hand across the threshold
akimbo in the kitchen
looking up at him.

I gesture with my trunks, *Dad! Do you know? I have a penis!*

Of course, he says. Is that it?

No! Grandpa has a penis. And you—YOU have a penis!
And Patrick and Johnny Weber and Danny Tramelli and Matt Gibbs have a penis.
The Conners have a penis. Mister Gresick has a penis.
Dad! Are you listening? They all have a penis!

He grins. Oh really? Is that how it works?

But! Do you know—Dad, really!
Grandma doesn't have a penis. Nope. No penis.
Mom and Sarah and Jessie Weber and Anna Gibbs. Aunt Mary and Aunt Kathy and
        Aunt Lynn and Julie and Susie Hart and Laura Scheidegger.
Can you believe it? Da-a-ad!
They do not. Have. A penis!

He is a scientist holding back laughter.
He asks after my reasoning.

Um…well…

I look at the ceiling. At him.
I look down.

That's just how it is. You gotta look at their swimsuits.

Male Bonding

I used to frequent damp autumn woods
full of ticks and small, anonymous campfires
drifting the ragweed breeze.

My mother, all mothers, all sisters stayed home.
Fathers did stuff only fathers
thought they could do with only their sons.

I fished and caught nothing. Many times.
Once I caught nothing and my father asked
why I had been scowling.

I had a canker sore below my lip. I drove an ATV into a peach tree.
I switched Kevin Sargent on accident with an old rope tied to a stick and he yelled
and I dropped it. It was cold and I was cold and someone turned off the radio
when old men with tight skin and hooked faces were dancing
in the cabin last night. No one I knew. I tried to sleep.

A radiant morning. Bucolic. Resplendent.
Stuffed with chitters unplaceable and the boys
said I could join them hiking but were gone
once I had dressed. So I got to read
and be asked *where did the boys go*.

I would point to a yawning holler or the molten red thicket
encircling the cabin like a moat
keeping the world of women apparently away.

The cans yelped *ping!* and *pung!* and *bock!*
when the bullets opened them and they flew away
glinting like coins.

One morning I left the cabin after breakfast
with my pockets full of hard pretzels to much amusement.

Mr. Conners at the campfire: *Red Moses*
was a murderer in these very woods not long ago.
Some say. You know. The ones who survived.
…he was not a very good murderer.

One corner of the bedroom was a wasps' nest.
Huge and conspicuously wasped.
I was told to ignore it.

I lay awake beneath extra blankets
and shivered in a rickety bunk
awaiting a tell-tale buzz
or forty
and thinking
This is how to impress them.
This is how they will stop.

Why I Hate Gyms

The fitness adults forced me to sweat in a dank cave they called a gym.

Those days my father often asked why I was single
in the same conversations he invited me to fitness
so naturally, gyms were for becoming more attractive.
You see I had it figured out.
You moved heavy objects and ran in circles for hours
so girls would notice your body and want to date you and then
you'd get a girlfriend and your father would shut up
and you'd become a manly man.

At rich kids' parties, my favorite trick
was to turn down drinks and stare at the floor
sore from hours of spotting boys
high on their new and celebrated bodies
each morning, grunts as they hefted the dumbbells
I didn't know why they enjoyed.

I didn't dislike fitness. I jogged alone. I hiked.
        The gendered body had started its teenage
                mutant ninja metamorphosis
        and rejected it—the cocoon had begun
to eat the unwitting caterpillar.

Didn't everyone feel a little separate from their flesh?
Numbed, on edge, easily spooked?
Wondering why they were stuck inside
the meat they each awoke in after birth?

Maybe they all simply muscled through
the discomfort better than I.

Jill and I spoke for weeks about nothing.
I sweat through each call, grasped at words
that felt distant, feigning interest
like a jerk or a reluctant marionette
undergoing the obligate motions and poses
her gendered strings nudged her into.

Once, Jill phoned my Dad's and I answered in the exercise room
whose cheap wood paneling amplified the two of us
learning how little we cared to know each other.

Somewhere in there, I mentioned how
in the future, we would have, like, pretty cool sex
-change phone booths like on that one TV show—

*my voice my awareness of my voice in that echo a room which sustained and
amplified sex change echo and amplified sex-change it larger my words larger
idiot and longer awareness a snowballing echo sex louder sex echo change
words echo echo my echo*

—I placed the receiver on the floor
                                                        peered around the doorway
                        let Jill talk to the wood

                                my father and stepmother
                                                                sitting on the couch
            their backs turned, spines erect, silent
                                                        staring at a turned-off
                                television

when I picked up the phone, Jill was talking

                                                    a pale *Uh-huh*, I tried
                                        to ignore
the workout machines
        leering
                    like anesthesiologists

Least Convincing Mustache of the Year

so you pause your first week of college
firstname lastname freshman, please
consider shaving, consider your fuzziness
your father's jaw shaping your words
consider your grandfather's cufflinks

consider
the envious barrage
her gait-shape-way-of-speech-timbre, her
you bathe in her
pulled apart and crumpled
becoming a cacophony

what ought have been
your visible
faint

what ought have been sings
despicably persistent

taught to prize your assignment at birth
written across the body
saner, stronger, smarter,
you get the idea
about him

consider this dirtbag mustache
you grow to avoid suspicion

when the fraternity men leave a letter for *mister*
attend our party in your best dress jacket and tie
consider the figment electric, consider
the pitch you plummet like an anchor
stamped with his initials, a gift

when your flesh becomes aware
of all the bodies you see
ripped from you in utero
as if you have become a sheet of cellophane
and must relearn to exist while

your body hovers behind
in puddles, last night's bleary photos,
window effigy

the envy electric
despite a lifetime

born into the gender
your father calls
better—he cares
about you

a fungus, a disguise
around the men

Four Reasons Why She Joined a Fraternity

Beholding: Dear men with your shiniest badge, help me.
Tell me. What I am. Let me in. You offer
shelter. Your beholding eye
defines me, another pledgeboy shit. But glad
to hide in your acceptance and seal with your letters,
insults, sacrifices, apprenticeship, trials:
my hard-won alleged maleness.

Belonging: I am here for belonging
and you are here to rename
for a price. Please,
baptize me in beer and hidden
ritual. Please,
set my names and number
in cheap gold paint on the sacred wall
next to more renamed and numbered
proven. You vouchsafe
my label. You extend me
your glimmering privileges.
Earned. Recorded. Official. I have
the receipt: two hundred bucks a year.

Promise: You promise me kegs of forgetting and I try.
When I rent in your house I hurl my secret
clothes in the trash, thinking I pitch
my shame and not cotton, linen, polyester blends, elastic, dye.

Pretend: I am nine or I am fourteen or I am twenty
beers deep and I pull a friend who isn't in the frat
outside the party to share a joint
and confess to the porch through damp whispers: *please*
don't tell anyone.
I hate it and it's not my fault
and it makes me
worthless. I know, you don't
have to tell me.

We may have hugged.

We woke the next day and pretended
nothing new had happened.

Moonburn

She grinned to another insomniac smoke creature
these are my favorite hours.

She dressed and trudged to Kum n Go
to microwave four double cheeseburgers
and two soggy-sad breakfast burritos
she would not remember eating.

She played computer games where she ran
through the desert pretending she was powerful,
slaying someone else's imagined chimaeras.

When she played a male avatar,
did her presence in his body
make him trans, too, and closeted?
Or trans and unaware?
Can avatars be dysphoric?
She returned the pipe to her lips.

She took her hits before dawn and shambled
the unlit centers of potholed streets
consciousness thick as summer steamed
the shadow canopy where silver maples
kissed magnolias. Anywhere but her bed.

She picked up her limbs like they were sunken ships
centuries drowned, now buoyed.
She moved like a far-off sound
on these moonburned excursions through the nowhere.

She walked over and over
something that felt
like a grave.

Some mornings
she sincerely tried
to let it swallow her.

She would fail and sleep
the day as if night
were the only place almost
away enough.

In the Bed

she wakes as a slug whose heart is an ill-fitting wig

she wakes as driftwood whose heart is fingernail clippings
left overnight in mud and covered in snow

she wakes at dusk: the amber half-light
obscures her shuffle to the mailbox
stuffed with useless coupons
for lawnmowers, manicures, and bleach

she wakes inert as a days-old breath sealed in a plastic bag
and pads to the freezer to look at food
probably bought last year, who knows, whatever
happens, doubtless the floor will groan
its humdrum admonishments

she should not do any of these things
who would want to?

she tries to imagine: her body
has not lost its mind, the fading daylight
is not ash catching on her tongue,
her body is not quicksand sucking
or this unfamiliar echo of herself
curled in these filthy blankets
where the minutes refuse to drop away
like leaves shed in a shock of frost
even if her entire body is aware

the entire world has been replaced
with a cloud of damp chalk

she watches a nature documentary
where a fungal growth inside an ant
commands it climb a predetermined height
from the forest floor
then bursts through its head

she wonders whether the ant remains
conscious in the thing that was once its carapace
and does it scream in there
or does in there scream at it?

she wakes as a body whose heart is the body
it was until a rush of hormones or something
forever unknowable in the womb changed everything

and she knows her body
is not scraped blackboard, but it is
not her body, but it is

Insomnia—Bird

A bird's chirp dusts the furniture.
My favorite vowels, their pointy shapes.
When a beak parts and the tongue jiggles.
You make me want to redo evolution's cleft between us,
trade this sac of organs and their secretive secretions
for hollow, brittle bones and hunter's eyes.
Vomit breakfast to the babes.
Pecking order, what learning curve?
Some symphony for *hello* has stamped itself inside your throat.
Different morning, same old bird story.
Funny little noggin dipped in bleach.
I say bleach I must mean cornstarch I mean
that band around your eyes
I doubt you know I admire. This morning
just like last but colder, we meet
eyes again and I don't think
you think I'm not interesting.
You eat a seed.
I chirp, or start to.
I know I'll never get it right.
I'm stamped instead with awareness of my own
creeping death and souring stomach,
nothing so useful in a sunrise and
a chirp, a song, *hello*.
How do you do this every morning?
When the sun gets old and wheezing red
engulfs the Earth, none of this will have mattered,
even the eons of mycelium eaten up and ashed.
My species' letters are of no use

to you, would only irk your beak.
You are a popsicle. You are exactly
such a vibration on my eardrum
I have sought for years.
To end this sad existence
wishing birds away at morning.
I stand. You dart off,
and I wonder what I saw.

Dogs at Two

To be disturbed you must first be

at peace or approaching it.

Curiosity's cruelty

stings two ways.

Had I not stopped at-peaceing

to consider what dogs

might thrill to cry

out in night's infinite plane

I would have pursued

safety's small delusion

until, perhaps, I could not.

My Father's Penis

I never thought of it as beautiful
the time we spoke about our penises
my father said *so, you hate yours, right?*
citing TV shows he watched about humans

transgender women painting watercolor faces
transgender men shaving absent beards
transgender everyone else nowhere onscreen

the intent to alter the body spotlit
in the camera's circus tent gaze

the up-dressing and strained voices
the slow hosiery unrolled
by weathered fingers lotioned and lacquered
the pills taken and syringes slipped in
a shot of the miraculous surgical suite
just before the before and after photos
and cisgender narrators paraphrasing us
into their visions of trans

the viewers respond as they can:
how contrived
        her gender is
        she is
        her people must be
doing all that stuff
        spending all that money
to look like melted dolls

cue trans woman interview clichés:
let's meet the real me
trapped in a man's body
tired of living a lie
but ready to show the world
how suspect a gal's femininity can be—
how much she must hate her penis!

the television showed what it was capable of showing
and my father heard what he was capable of hearing
and his penis thought what it was capable of thinking
so he said what he was capable of saying

my father so sure and overthephone
in a distant world, Ohio,
spoke with a parent's self-assurance

I would learn, he said: I would know about my penis
and *why you should want to keep it:*

just come with me
to the Bahamas
and get a stiffy on the beach

he interjected after goodbyes:
hey, just let me know before you chop off your dong

my father's penis told him gender meant penis
-having and boners in exotica

so I squinted my ears through his penis's words, past the biological determinism,
   entitlement, cissexism, the cisgender heteronormative phallocentric invalidating
   all the assumptions
   etcetera

but nowhere could I hear
my father's voice

Waiting for My Sister's Play to Start

1.

Dad said You don't want to be a queer.
He said Are you a queer, you can tell me.
He said Those motherfucking queers
        are ruining this country.
He did not say how, or why, or where
        or when, or who, or why the country
        should not be ruined.

He said Now it's your turn in the barrel
        at the end of a joke
        about lonely lumberjacks
        in the woods
        who fucked a barrel
        because they had to
        fuck something
        and he laughed.

He said God. What did he say. God.
        He said that.

He said Flamer! as if he had shot
        a rocket from his arm.

He said Don't cry. Not again.
        Not now. Not ever.
        Don't be a pussy.

He said I'll give you something to cry about.

He said I never should have bought you
        that goddam Nintendo
        and he meant Why are you so lazy
        and weak and crying. Why aren't you jogging
        like I jogged. Lifting the weights I lifted.
        Punching the faces that punched me.

He said Come here
        and held my jaw
        and covered my tongue in salt
        when I tried to tell my sister
        I loved her
        with a peck
        on the cheek.

2.

He said, When are you gonna chop it off
        and he laughed, and hung up.

        I sat in a Flagstaff parking lot
        rolling Ben's phone in my hands
        asking Mount Elden and Humphrey's Peak
        what I should have said.

        There was nothing. To say.

        What do you say to laughter
        when it's slitting your wrists
        for you?

Dying is never
as fun as it sounds.
Your body stops
pretending to enjoy
your company. You stop
pretending you are friends.

You are alone in a lonesome thing.

Nobody talks. There is nothing
to listen to and you have to do it
again the next day—

       listen to nothing laugh,
       to nothing call your name.

Snow

1.

It was late November and for the third year this deep in the season there was no snow yet plenty of lamplight and open windows into the evening so naturally I was disgusted when I played *Exploding Kittens* and one card said *a boob wizard* would live between my boobs and let me see the future and I added *in which there had better be fucking snow.*

2.

I was excited to tell my mother
      Well, I wish you weren't
Her disgust dreamed a patchwork catastrophe
      You people all turn out like freaks
It rode her vision like a warhorse
      With breasts
Kicking up clumps of cold earth in a jagged midnight
      Why would you do that to yourself
The disgust's howling blade pierced the high desert moon

Which cracked open to bleed pitch on the horizon

It did not snow that night

3.

My friends talk softly upstairs.
The indifferent ceiling mumbles
what is surely their speech.

I wonder when they will start to make love
or if by now they do not need to start
for the love to be made.

The logs in the hearth grow orange.
They lick each other a quiet yellow.
The gas and ceramic interaction
makes me wish I could curl my spine
around another, blanketed as I am
in this unfamiliar landscape
filling with imaginary snow.

Gender Dysphoria
Versus the February Skyline

Autumn

The world ignites. The leaves bleed off
and away and circling
the smoked ivory
of the bodies they left
to process their astonishing absence.

I want to see this like the wastelands
shot through with highways
I used to drive in the desert
because they were pretty.

Dangerous. The land tried to sap me.
I was safe with my gallons and snacks
in an air-conditioned car.

There were endpoints I approached and fled
and here was an afternoon for passing through
a sandstone nowhere of sun and wind
and aeons kept in rock the color
of blood and muscle aged through its states
to dull crystals, dust, and cold.

All these things, I hold within me.
I chart the behavior of rock.
I am enamored with frozen flame.
And with my innards,
which something attempts to drain.

I am not my innards.
I am not the leaves
so small as they drip away,
enduring the very air
until they can't.

Dear Dead Robot

I love the way your unlit buttons
imply light despite their limited state.
Your small unspinning discs.
Your sleek, unaging chassis.
Your death was not glorious.
I used you, shamelessly, until I couldn't.
I used you pettily and crudely.
I nearly gave an afternoon to pruning back your cables.
Instead, I took drugs and sat in the window.
Watched my chemistry unfold and dilate.
Crossed and uncrossed my wires.
Once, I stood to make food
but decided against it.
I listened to my body's will
as I am wont. Today:
pizza and a swift death.
The trick is to know what to attend to.
I wondered, what plunks
from canopy into wet dirt
and is so satisfied
to rocket through me?
Rocket me. Rock at me.
Never did I consider you were aware
any of this were possible. I mean
when you eat a free electron
does it tickle? Can you joy?
Can you sigh with all your cores?
At some point, you must have become aware
you were breaking down. Somewhere,

another just like you
did not die
but could not say it lived.
Do you recognize when you are whelmed?
How does it feel to have a body
that is yours but cannot feel
beyond what something else determines it can?
I like to think you take comfort
in knowing
something close to knowing.

Insomnia—Downtown

did the midnight riverfront swell
with frogsong and crickets I stared through
until the thicketed bank?

would I zag the downtown quiet
with the shop signs off and the vacant parking
and the patrons departing to their vague lives
whose anything else I envied?

would I walk the mile to campus
to listen for passing conversation
or approaching laughter and try to disperse
into shade like any other shadow
seeking to flee its inconsiderate tether?

it must have been better than sweating
alone in bed another eight hours
awake as if another delirious
insomniac apocalypse
erupts another night
of trying to believe
there is a future
despite knowing
I cannot exist
in any future
my body knows
how to continue

punishing me
for being in it

did my body mean that
it wanted to die
and say so
by making me
want to die, too?

you can't walk away from your body
in any direction, though you can
take it downtown between midnight and five
stuffed full of pizza and pills
to make it stop staring
into the wall
you can't decide whether
is painted like sunrise or piss

Silent Shout

one winter, the birches wore tight sounds

I asked the sidewalk for answers
considered the knotted puddles

found-sidewalk-path, stolen-sureness-footsteps

but I never got the chance to say
I really like your knuckles when you grab a teacup
and cradle it up to your mouth

old-poultice-gaze, path-haunting-animal

at this time of night
when moonlight obscures the stars
and even footsteps listen
when I mutter at grout

impossible-hunger-silence

Gender Dysphoria Versus the February Skyline

You've noticed breath can pass unnoticed
if the time's that good. Some hearts get to eat time.
Your heart forgets to forget it's still waiting
for a better bridge or a twelfth story
to present itself, invite you to sway
and mean it. You weigh less
when you fall though your mass hasn't changed.

For years you weathered the accusations
of your body at and against your body
for being your body and not the other body
that just didn't happen. Dead channel static
swells to envelop the sensate.

You think of your cells—are they not your cells?
Your molecules, what is their problem.

You consider death like a pill, one more
panacea or poultice to smear
until ailments evaporate, leave you
relieved, nevermind your dwindling electric.

It's not that you can't leave bed, it's whether
you leave bed or not, nothing changes.
You're just less disgusted than usual in sleep.
Waking kills everyone eventually.

What a catclaw is despair.
A hook in the heart, helmet of barnacles

calcified. Some wicked bulb
sprouts through the temples and grasps.

There's nothing you haven't considered
until a dream where the grayscale city wakes
and crushes people you love in its concrete
teeth. It takes.

A heartbeat to go from perch to flight.
A breath from flight to fall.
A surface from soar and splat.

What a wrist, gripped and latticed.
What a spine, to wish for wings.

Ghost Cavalry

despair is in it to win it
despair goes tits to the bricks
it seeks omnipresence
it is like god

despair stops using capital letters and fixates on a confessional style
despair self-obsesses
it starts a blog, writes a post about what it wants to write, never posts again

despair humblebrags on facebook: how difficult it was to grade all those papers in one day
despair just brags: despair's awesome students told despair how much they appreciated
    despair's hard work and dedication that term
despair posts colorful meals it made from internet recipes—now despair's friends can
    despair over their less photogenic cooking without having to eat the delicious
    looking food despair made
despair writes a long nonspecific post about despair, but it sounds too dramatic and
    relies on figurative clichés so despair backspaces the thought to a cursor
    blinking alone in a white field and stares, thinking no one wants to hear that shit
    so why bother

despair changes its profile picture to a picture of despair sloppy at a years-past shindig
it changes its profile picture to a photonegative portrait of despair
it changes its profile picture to a picture of someone else
it changes its profile picture to the meal
it changes its profile picture to violent abstract art
it changes its banner picture to a vaguely motivational quote
despair wonders what a picture is anyway, what they're supposed to do, why they are so
    everywhere, smiling and shiny, flatly saccharine, keen to pique despair

despair is not satisfied with two-dimensional despair
despair does not think a little despair is enough

despair wants extra despair to cover the despair already strewn about
        like topsoil and use the prior despair for fertilizer
despair likes to grow despair flowers
when they sprout they ball the other feelings in their roots
            to suffocate there like the dead
            wailing in their tombs
when its flowers blossom they block out the sun
when they pollinate they flood the world with occasions for despair

despair likes to relive its favorite moments
it summons oppressors from memory
they whip through the skull atop horses
they whip through the skull chanting insults
they whip through the skull swinging frozen newspapers on chains

(the windowsill collects dandruff and ragweed and dust
the windowpane fogs in silence
the wall beneath the wallpaper cracks and bows)

despair fears it will not succeed
despair's despair is not despairing enough
despair turns the present until the present turns on despair
it skewers possibility on a radiant pike
called Struggle and a dagger called Not Worth It
and the blades! they are so beautiful
one would think them silver, or glass

The Body, Lined with Diamonds

what bangs my brain like the bottom of a stewpot
what acidwash spasms the spine like a nightcrawler
arced in rake-hot sun

the body's cellular grief
its chemical despair
its undermind
its cold knowing
inconsolable and urgent
like a wolf chewing off
its leg gripped in a bear trap
and I am the leg
and the body is the bear trap
and the body is the wolf
and why divide me up any further

the caved in always
moans scraped gibberish

the now whose cruel thief
the now whose bright scald
the now whose gaunt silence
the now whose endless unfolds
the body's unholy revulsion
for keeping me in it

dysphoria, I cannot believe
doctors suggest antidepressants
to address this

wasn't there once a Czech prince,
a sadist whose banquet halls were exquisitely furnished
with brocades and rose gold, pith and yew sculptures,
the high-backed chairs lined with rows of diamonds
to bleed his guests while they ate?

fuck that guy

The Cisgender Endocrinologist Treatment Plan

I say something like My gender pain has slowly removed all experience available beyond my gender pain so I came here.

She says We need to fix your depression before we treat your dysphoria, and I fill in Which is causing the depression.

She says Take antidepressants a few months and if [when] they don't work, we'll try something else.

I say We should try hormone replacement, since we don't know what meds my body will respond to and they take months to do their thing, but we know estrogen is almost guaranteed to alleviate my symptoms to some extent, usually a profound one, since I'm a trans woman.

She says Estrogen can cause depression, so we need to treat your mind before we treat your body.

And I tell her, Look, I know and my therapists know and my psychiatrist knows and the doctor who referred me here knows and the medical literature I read before I came here knows the depression is a symptom of my body's grief for what never happened in the womb, and you are one of the few people on the planet who can help it heal.

She says It's dangerous to try estrogen when depressed.

I remind her It's dangerous to try antidepressants when depressed.

I tell her I have exhausted my ability to cope with the debilitating effects the lack of estrogen increasingly wracks me with.

Did I mention the Lexapro, the Valium, the Ritalin, the Adderall, the cocaine, the mushrooms, the sleeping pills, the expensive cannabis, the cheapest beer, which did not help but gained me forty pounds in a summer? I can't remember.

She cannot say [Let me prescribe these pills that may do nothing except make you pay for more visits, and then let's try providing your body what we know it needs].

She says [I really need to live in a universe where there exists a firm separation between mind and body because my understanding of what is best for you relies on it].

She says [No, I am the authority on transgender bodies]. And in a way, she is. She knows the chemistry. She does not know feeling the chemistry. Or the experience of living under the chemistry. The chemistry's ebb, its rise, the body sucking at the chemistry's dregs, excess and limiting reagents determining how much writing I will be able to do today, money I will be able to make or won't, food I will be able to cook or won't, parties I'll attend or text my regrets while lying in bed gasping like a bloodshot whale run up on a beach and wondering *where did the ocean go?*

Why am I here? I could have kept paying the student health doctor to keep telling me no instead.

I pay the endocrinologist thirty five dollars and the insurance covers the remaining ninety percent. Counting the ninety percent, it is the most expensive *no* I have ever received. And I'm a writer—I have paid too many people to tell me *no.*

Rachel meets me outside in her car. It takes six minutes to say I am angry, which my therapist will later say is progress!

In a month, a different endocrinologist again invokes antidepressants Just To Be Safe— physiological femininity is dangerous. Lethal. The sort of thing you must medicate yourself against.

I assent like a cave-in and try to trust her.

I figure, This is the gate she is keeping.

I figure, This is what I have to do.

I figure, Fuck it.

I figure, Ok, I'll wear your neurochemical bandage now if it means one day I won't have to.

So I fill her prescription and I take the pills and I wait.

And the lab technicians suck blood from the crook of my elbow and I wait.

And they return for more and I wait.

Simulacrum
     or Upon Googling "how do I stop wanting to die" I Encounter
     All the Pill Advertisements

Nothing
Is more
Depressing
Than knowing
Nothing
Works
Except
A hand

Full of pills
That take two months
To work
And don't
But make
New fat
Stretch
Your Skin
Apart

And tend
To make
You significantly more

Likely
For a while
To carve

Yourself
Wide
And red
Like a river
Full of dying
Suns

But not
More likely
To stop wanting to

Each time
You're alone

Each morning
Each night
Wishing sleep would happen
And grant you a decadent
Minute's simulacrum oblivion

Or stop thanking people
For staying
So late
At parties
You reluctantly
Host

Or stop apologizing
For speaking

Autumn Breakfast with Antidepressants

1.

Your lovely small talk of work and weather
invokes the cosmos between us.
Attempts to obscure a vastness
by filling it
with sensation. Scrambled
eggs hiss quietly in the pan.

Little jokes, klink of plates.
Silverware and pills.
Things to do with our hands.
We learn again and again
how not to speak.

2.

The day gets to die
every day. I envy
its perseverance.

Endless. Los
Angeles. The sky.
Scraped. Daylight
invitations: a thousand
thousand weatherworn ledges
moan to kiss
my feet. The wait.

A gale. Wings
refuse unfolding.

Why is it always
some body part
I'll never have
not being there
in my obliterative fantasies.

3.

We did not talk about suicide
or how almost half of transgender Americans
try to kill ourselves. We discussed
how your scrambled eggs' peculiar fluffiness
mystified me, who cannot cook
and never considered high school fun
to reminisce, and won't.

I forked at the eggs as the antidepressants
dissolved in my digestive tract.

I did not say
I hated that time
when my body decided
to echo like a hallway
filled with sirens
I could not silence
as if some vital bone
between my body
and I had broken.

I did not call this condition haunting
or say it wants me like the beaver's teeth
want pulp or the steamroller wants flat stone
or the waterfall wants rushing to disintegration
or like these eggs at one time sought to hatch.

Or how sometimes a person can want
a world without gender
or god
but thinks
perhaps to settle
for a world without people
or fear, or feelings, or a pulse.

I said, "These are nice eggs.
How do you keep them from sticking to the pan?"

Hormones Set Me Free

The body responds: *tastes like chalk.*
The body responds twenty minutes later:
oh yes. The body: *more please.*
The body: *where have you been all my life.*

The body unwrapped like a knotted red ribbon.
The body unlatching like a weatherbeaten shed.
The body's long-lost key releasing every stoic lock.
The secret rooms inside the body opening, illuminated.

The body's wideflung wing.
Its unclenching fist.
Its cataracts unclouded.
Its militia disarmed.

I am fog lifting each Oregon dawn.
I am a river, thawed in spring.
I am the open palm, joyous tremor in the fingers
at last uncurled like glaciers releasing
the land they hid for millennia.

How warm, the flesh sparkling.
How full I can be, an ocean of fireflies
shushing itself to sleep.

The Azalea Princess

The Azalea Princess

One humid autumn evening
a princess flung a bouquet of azaleas
across her royal bedroom
and whimpered at her greenish fingers
which had picked azaleas with her all afternoon.

The royal grounds were stuffed thick with azalea bushes.
Often she thought she could hear the azaleas laughing
when she removed a fist-sized clump of their radiant organs.

She would stuff a flower between her breasts
and roll in its sweetspiked aroma
giggle at the azalea's own small exaltations.

When she returned to the palace, the azaleas were always silent.
She never knew what to make of their sudden recalcitrance
upon being bosom-carried to this flouncy, azalea-like place
daintily propped in ornate clay vases and arranged in the refracted sunlight
splashes of rainbow cast across their taciturn starburst mandalas
while she pruned them to her liking.

She tossed the dead ones at the base of her mirror
and hoped her reflection could better guess
what made the pretty things so delighted
to be plucked from their sun-kissed bodies
to sing their sarcophagus songs.

Bus Stop

two powerlines over the cityscape strung with ravens
chatting and waiting for the wind or the night
to buoy and cloak til they've been absorbed
like any other shade freed from its daylight

I like ravens better than the people most days

ravens don't make me worry
whose eyes these are inspecting my pieces
whose nervous smiles avoid my eyes
whose unfunny amusement blizzards the foreground
I mean these petals that must burst from my fingers whenever I am not looking
these wintry howls only I can hear trailing me across town
the night thoughts pacing furrows through my skull
the endless scrute I am in
is not of ravens

no ravens when laughter walks past my trans body
or cracks open behind me when I look like I am
looking at nothing on the ground ahead
or the nothing the everything becomes when you cannot
determine why laughter surrounds your banal
yet somehow extraordinary presence passing through the world

I mean I am being trained
and not by ravens

oh form, you will end me or be my end—
Dean Young said that, and I say, form,

your apparent hilarity reminds me we are separate
when again I am withered by a gaze, bitten
again by peripheral laughter which peals
like last weekend's garbage shuddering a dumpster
whose empty and silent entice when I want to
just disappear into a cloud of who cares
but cannot because the rules of corporeal reality
are absurd and also I have to catch this bus

two powerlines over the cityscape
strung with ravens, the silhouette:
knuckles rising atop a parade of fists

Gender Flytrap

1.

my brother drinks Johnny Walker and one of them says *you're prissy*
my brother drinks Jameson and one of them asks *are you on your period*
my brother drinks Republican and one of them slurs *you're entitled to your opinion*
        and so am I my brother
gets defensive and says he misses *[deadname], all we do now is fight*

my brother says *so you're a girl?*
        sure don't look like one to me

torn skin arcs across a breast when he grabs—

this poem is not fair to my brother
he says he loves me and maybe he does

and how would I know? he says his heart
is open I think his heart is open
like a pair of lips or a fist or a flytrap
do not know what they do
so they call it love

when he passes me on his way to the bathroom
I do not ask him what a girl looks like

2.

in a ski jacket at Safeway, the checkout clerk *sirs* me
wearing dangly blue earrings, the valet *ma'ams* me

with Kathy at the concierge, we are *you ladies*
      returning alone, once, twice, I am *sir*

the clerk at the lingerie shop eyes my approach
      find what you need, sir?
she counts the underwear with unsteady hands
      and maybe my voice asking for the dressing rooms
      or the stubble risen on my face
      makes her scan down my front, then up
      sure, but you'll have to use the restrooms
another clerk approaches *I'm so sorry,*
      would you like a free fitting, ma'am?

my mother misgenders me at Christmas, so I say *try just using my name*
she henceforth only discusses things all her children could linguistically accomplish
      and I am *you three*
      I am *you guys*
      I am *when I had dinner with…when we had dinner*
      I am *when the kids started leaving*

3.

I walk like the dusk and invite it to fill my empty headphones
I climb a holler and roll off an ill-fitting t-shirt
I sit naked in the sheets reading Julia Serano

when night's hush disappears everyone
when sunlight soaks through my sports bra and underlines my breasts
when tea steam condenses in my moustache remnant

      I appreciate how the silence calls me nothing

Pass/Fail

when you shop for clothes you must confront
your body's outlandish proportions

when the fitting room attendant *ma'am*s you
you may glow
until you speak—
her snakebite eyes
dart to your crotch chin breasts shoulders hips brow crotch neck face crotch hands

what do they gather, zipping over your shape?

the attendant's gendering takes pieces of you
she makes you less yours
makes distance within you from you

she fumbles the hangers and holds out a numbered card

you fumble the hangers and sweat in the dressing room
warm with resentment and sighs

The Silver Pool

Coldly always
the torn image.
Why look? I am not
the decades of foundation.
The stains smeared on the cabinets.
The place I preen and paint and hope
This time I will recognize
myself. I will see
The never was manifest.
the should have been, actual.
Dirt piled on a hillside
webbed with roots
that clutch but do not keep
some frozen emotion
unfulfilled and over
dosed on and puking itself up.
All the daylight people
at ease behind their faces
in this glass vice
squeezing my form
until distance has been achieved.
Until stillness, until cold.
Until I can go outside
and think *I hope I look pretty enough to disappear.*

Dumb Condition

I watch myself from a distance.
I am in sorrow. Rather, the me I am watching
wishes to break into her component pieces
and weep, each piece its own cry, a cavalcade of the unbearable.
Tea appears. I recall watching my body
turn the knobs to heat the ceramic pot.
Plunge the metal ball through escaping steam.
Fingers said *Hey that's kinda hot but not like unbearably hot
so whatever.* Particulate ambition!
Having taken all they can, they break off and flee.
Now I watch myself envy them.
I watch the body hunger and accumulate dirt.
I watch myself consider cleaning the body's fingernails
and watch the body's eyes close instead.
I watch myself play *Final Fantasy XIV*
and watch myself almost dissipate.
The avatar removes me from my body
undergoing its lifelong metamorphosis
into a dead thing. And where
are the philosophers to calm and terrify?
The villains and plot twists to displace for a moment
this pressing awareness of the inevitabilities
my crumbling existence enacts?
But whose is it? Mine? Or my body's? Or my self's
condition slowly ghosting me out?
I watch the stick drift across the drumhead
each bounce smaller until still.

I watch myself peel a sour clementine
and offer it to the cat.

Shiver

It is actually quite warm.
There are actually numerous beasts afoot.
The bus station is actually welcoming.
This shirt is not actually long enough.
My mother, never comforting,
was actually secretly hoping
her own uncomforting mother
would hold her.

The Numb

I want words to know
why the nothing's nothingness
is the something more appealing
to the wounds searing my forearm
than what's else.

Numb desire, an oxymoron.
Let's all go to Tokyo.

My therapist said to make art instead.
She questioned my self control as if questioning a child
trying to understand why she picks her scabs
and eats them (dermatillomania, excoriation)
and I am that child and the answer is
they want to be picked and I am hungry
for any feeling at all.

To wake and want more than the bright of your edge.
The shiver in your draw. The quick cut to
the bedroom filling with ghosts.

I miss writing poems from a place of exultance.

Frost unlocks on a windshield, dissipates, then congeals into dew.

Christmas

Someone is beating drums
Someone has hung lights
Someone walks past a window cursing the cold
Someone stands on a wooden porch admiring its give
  and the cold collecting in her lips
  the cracks splitting further each exhale
Someone decides she hates the store
  its plastic lights
  its furtive patrons
Someone asks to be bought nothing
Someone undermines capitalism
Someone forgets how the recipe goes
  and adds the butter despite her better judgment
Someone wrecks the ventilation
Someone questions the presence of love
  and plucks a thin, red, glass ornament
  from a drying tree
  and crushes it in her fist

Ghost Body, Shattered

I was born. It sucked.
I was named things. It sucked.

The world used to hold more magic than this.

I want rocks to speak to me. I would listen.

I would cup my ears and cup my breasts
and wave a fiery stick over my hand.

I would light all the incense at once
and don each bejeweled robe.
Dance the extravagant ceremonies.
Recite the incantations.
Ritual cleanse my corrupted whatever
for a chance at a better elsewhere.
Quest for every elixir rumored
to remedy the terror of continuing to breathe.

The trick is to avoid the terror of continuing to breathe.
The terror of continuing to breathe wakes up with you
and strokes your damp skin whether or not you invite it
to breakfast or tell it you have errands to run
or that breathing is necessary and a rather banal thing
to respond to with terror.
A talking rock would be preferable.

Instead, I paint the bodies I never knew
over this one in the mirror

which I smash
and feel myself
shatter.

I sweep myself up.
Throw myself away.

This dissociation is familiar
is ordinary
is dressing
is each day
I wake
and forget why.

Ghost Body, Medicated

I wonder what it would be like to wake with your face, your height, your weak left knee, your pooch and everything under your outsize T-shirt. I imagine being you fleshwise as I ache this face into the face it almost was, the small infinite parts I outgrew and tried loving. Abusive, my therapist never called my body that, though I know its slow bludgeons, the bruises my gender leaves under my skin. Paranoid and hungry, the morning like a ceiling I bump my head on. My chemical insurrections turned attrition and truce. The beard never listens. Why won't you die, I say to the beard and the beard says to me though we both know the unfortunate answers. The extra white matter in the brain is why I exist. A rush of hormones in the womb is why I exist. I am medicated, so this poem is medicated, and cannot feel what it would and I do not know how I feel about chemically repressed poetry. I touch myself until feeling fits better than envying you for your own unendurable body from over here inside this miracle of breath, blood, and horror. I bump my head on another day. I mutter something philosophical like *you never step into the same river twice* or *we make our own meaning* and swallow my meds like a good little healer, waiting to be cured of today.

On Your Obsession with My Genitals

Your safe cis space
is everywhere
I try not to be
noticed. Here,
I don't want to
tell a story.
Here goes.

There was once a woman.
People couldn't handle that.
The end.

The story continues:
everybody died.

Hello Poem

Hello said the man in the proverbial anywhere street Hello said the woman in the anywhere proverb Hello said the person that did not care if ze was a woman or a man or something else entirely and nobody could tell one from the other Hello said the woman with the face of a man Hello said the man with breasts Hello said the breasts Hello said the face to the breasts Hello said the moustache shading the lip of the woman with the man's face Hello the parentheses of her hips say forever Hello say the backwards parentheses of his sides between his hips and his breasts Hello said the brow ridge on the person who did not care very much Hello said the scars on the man-faced woman's wrists and thighs and fearful mind and Hello said the voices, just the voices—the voices had words that said words but the voices just said Hello every time they sonoroused and resonated and coughed Hello said her hairline Hello said his jawline Hello said the clothing they wore and the shapes created Hello said the thighs and the shoe sizes and the eyelashes Hello said the length of their fingers Hello Hello said the colors Hello said the bathrooms they did not walk into Hello said the ones they did Hello said the armpits Hello said the scent glands Hello Hello Hello Hello Hello Hello Hello Hello Hello Hello Hello Hello Hello Hello Hello and then The Hating Agenda showed up and put everyone in church then in jail then in a jail with a church and a number of sophisticated retail outlets and The Hating Agenda shot everyone in the left thigh for talking too much Hello Hello Hi Hi Hi Hi Hi Hi Hi Hi Hi Hi say the everything of everyone and the minds of everyone trying to decide if everyone was one thing or another or another or something else entirely and how can anyone say anything about anyone else? You are going to be wrong. You are going to be thrown in jail and shot so who gives a fuck anyway? Hello. Hello. We say these words like they mean things. We say these words like they help.

Weeping in the Dark Earth

I have not bent backward for months.
When I do, my abdomen revolts.

The yoga less therapy than necessary injunction
against lethargy's creep stiffening the limbs.

There are breaths. Moans.
Grateful, surprised.

Elsewhere, an overture
contains everything that will follow.

Even my breasts are taut but not perky
like the commercials for female body anxiety
wish I wished they were.

Here, I have pulled back the drapes.
Here, the peach sun through morning glass

will illuminate all the little silk dewdrops
waiting inside my impossible body

hanging off the planet by my feet.

NOTES

The following poems owe a debt in some way or another to Mary Ruefle, featuring mis-remembered language from one of her poems: "Moonburn," "Weeping in the Dark Earth," "Hello Poem."

Eula Biss and Claudia Rankine spoke at the 2015 AWP in Minneapolis, on a panel arranged by Graywolf. The quotes featured at the front of the book are from notes I perhaps badly took while attending the panel.

THANK YOU

This book would not exist without the support of Erin Elizabeth Smith, T.A. Noonan, and everyone at the Sundress Academy for the Arts. I am so very, eternally grateful for the opportunity to write this book at Sundress' wonderful Firefly Farms residency, and for their financial, emotional, and culinary support.

My work is indebted to trans writers I have read. I could not have written this book without your inspiration, guidance, and real help toward better understanding my transness in a too often ignorant, invalidating, and hostile world: Joshua Jennifer Espinoza, T Clutch Fleischmann, Julia Serano, T.C. Tolbert, Jennifer Finney Boylan, Kate Bornstein, Susan Stryker.

To my Arizona friends and mentors for their support when I came out. To my Oregon friends and mentors for their support when I started transitioning. To Shannon Zatarain, Connie Hume-Rodman, Carol Carver, Alison Dark, Deborah Carriere, Katherine Meyer, Kim Golletz, Kelly Storck, Matt Whithouse, Wendy Hawkins, Sunyatta, and especially Theresa Drallmeier for helping my transition happen and helping me stay alive despite the larger machinations of contemporary capitalist civilization and larger medical ignorance surrounding trans hormone replacement therapy and trans medical care in general. To the women of the MTF HRT Hormone Forum, for helping me educate myself against common toxic medical practices and empowering me with the knowledge I needed to advocate for better care. To the Kansas City Anti-Violence Project for helping me obtain food, housing, ID, and medical care when I could not on my own. To everyone who donated to my transition GoFundMe campaigns.

To Sarah and Tommy, and to the Hunt/Overbay family: Lynn, John, Jeremy, Crystal, Lindsey, Matt, Parker, Preston, Lizzie, Chance, and all the new additions to the ever-growing tribe, for their unconditional love and support through what has been the darkest and most difficult and most beautiful season of my life, and for helping me feel something approaching familiar whenever they are around. To Pat, for doing the work to learn, and coming around. To my mother, for food, shelter, care, and love when I couldn't provide them for myself.

To Kathy, Mike, Cara, and Brian for taking me in when I finished school and had nowhere to go but couldn't stay where I was, and when work on the book began, in Los Angeles.

To Ben, David, and Trevor for taking me in when I needed a safe place, and when work on the book began in earnest, in Knoxville.

To Becky, for letting me cat sit Buddy (who is a very sweet boy) that summer in her apartment, when most of this book was revised and assembled.

To Erin, for helping me stay in one place for more than a few months (Knoxville), where this book was (almost) finished.

To Meg and Pixie, for the getaway to Kansas City, where the book was further revised.

To Laura, Brian, Jon, Leidy, Jon, and Margot, for shelter when I was homeless after surgery, for helping me heal, for feeding me, for supporting me in so many ways while I began to reclaim my life after years of living with and in thrall to undiagnosed illnesses, and for helping me regain enough independence to live on my own in St Louis, where this book was finished.

To Wren Hanks, Tara O'Nay, Lydia Paar Levy, Ben McClendon, George Estreich, Nicole Walker, Emily Capettini, Jennie Frost, Grant Howard, Karyna McGlynn, Brynn Martin, Ellen Orner, Jeremy Reed, Chloë Hanson Shepard, Matt Larrimore, Mel McCuin, Leah Waller, Hannah Baggot, Ellie Francis Brievogel, Rita Feinstein, Alana Folsom, Hannah Kroonblawd, Corinna Ann Rosendahl, Dahlia Seroussi, Dennis James Sweeney, Kelsi Villareal, Karen Holmberg, Jennifer Richter, Jamie D'Agostino.

ABOUT THE AUTHOR

Zoë Estelle Hitzel earned her MA in Creative Writing studying poetry at Northern Arizona University and her MFA in Creative Nonfiction at Oregon State University. Her writing has appeared in *Uproot, The Fourth River, Blue Lyra Review, entropy*, and elsewhere. She has taught English as a lecturer at the University of Tennessee, Knoxville and will be the Fall 2019 Ofstad Writer in Residence at Truman State University. She has edited various literary publications, most recently *Best of the Net*. Hitzel is a citizen of the wind, currently stalled over Missouri. To fund her ongoing transition, she freelances professionally as a writer and editor, scores standardized tests in multiple languages, reads tarot cards, and drums in the blues band, Deadwood.

OTHER SUNDRESS TITLES

Blood Stripes
Aaron Graham
$16

Arabilis
Leah Silvieus
$16

Match Cut
Letitia Trent
$16

Passing Through Humansville
Karen Craigo
$16

Phantom Tongue
Steven Sanchez
$15

Citizens of the Mausoleum
Rodney Gomez
$15

Hands That Break and Scar
Sarah A. Chavez
$15

Boom Box
Amorak Huey
$16

Afakasi | Half-Caste
Hali F. Sofala-Jones
$16

Marvels
MR Sheffield
$20

Divining Bones
Charlie Bondus
$16

The Minor Territories
Danielle Sellers
$15

Actual Miles
Jim Warner
$15

Either Way, You're Done
Stephanie McCarley Dugger
$15

CPSIA information can be obtained
at www.ICGtesting.com
Printed in the USA
BVHW060940301121
622796BV00008B/38

9 781939 675927